PHOTOGRAPHIC NOTES
The photographs in this book were taken with motor-driven 35mm Pentax cameras.
The cameras were hand-held, helmet-mounted and remote-mounted on outboard stations of aircraft and from elevated positions on the ground. Remote camera operations were made by electronic release.
Focal lengths used in free fall were 17mm, 20mm, 28mm and 35mm, while the general photography utilised focal lengths from 17mm to 300mm. The two basic films were Kodachrome-X and Ektachrome-X. Use of high speed Ektachrome and Infra-red Ektachrome films were made where film speed or effect were required.

No tripods, light meters or electronic flash were used, as they penalise mobility. Exposures, with the primary film speeds of 64 ASA, were $\frac{1}{500}$ second at f4–f5.6 in bright sunlight, rule of thumb for late sunlight or overcast, and bracketing for unusual lighting.

SKIES CALL

© COPYRIGHT · ANDREW C. KEECH
FIRST EDITION JULY 1974

ISBN   0 9503341 0 3

PUBLISHED IN ENGLAND BY ANDREW C. KEECH
3022 PORTER ST N.W   WASHINGTON DC   20008   U·S·A
And at 'VANHALLA' WICKHURST RD
SEVENOAKS WEALD · KENT · ENGLAND

Printed by: Beric Press Ltd · Crawley · Sussex · England
Colour Separations by: Daiichi Seihan Co Ltd · Hong Kong.

SKIES CALL

PHOTOGRAPHED
AND WRITTEN BY
ANDY KEECH

DESIGNED AND
PRODUCED BY
J. PARTINGTON SMITH.

SKIES

The concept of this book, to try to define and express the spirit and nature of our sport, pictorially and textually, began on impulse in 1970, eventually involved forty thousand miles of travel and the culling of ten thousand slides to distill the essence of an image.

I would like to thank all those who supported all the operations involved:
Bill Bettum, for the construction of my camera mounts and continual maintenance on the camera's remote wiring;
Dave Holdredge, for his enthusiastic organisation of sequential formations;
The James Gang, who took me into their world of team precision;

CALL

Reg Guy and Dave Guinn, my longtime flying friends, who flew and jumped with me on peculiar projects, that must have seemed as pointless to them as they occasionally seemed fruitless to me;

Jerry Irwin, for his relaxed advice and cooperation on things photographically technical;

All the unnamed jumpers, who asked me to come along, trusting me to be up to my job.

I would also like to thank John ("P.S.") Partington Smith, of the British Star Team, for handling the layout of this book and allowing the production, to the point of printing, to be a completely in-family effort.

This book is for jumpers, about jumping, by jumpers.

Andy Keech

Parachuting as a sport is happily a fact, in spite of the improbable factors causing its development. Aircraft were not generally available to the man in the street till the end of the second world war, and parachutes not easily obtained till a large surplus was generated for the Korean war.

However, the most surprising and unexpected factor was man's ability to fly in the third element with his body alone. While he had ventured aloft in various lift-supported containers for several centuries, he nevertheless, still had to be in the container.

Even more surprising was man's speed and eagerness to learn a previously unknown form of body locomotion. It could not have been inherited, as people who fell long distances in the past, failed to produce off-spring. Yet, he learned that he could lie flat in the air with confidence after a mere 60 seconds of exposure to free flight. By the second minute of free fall he could execute simple turns and after 30 minutes could close vertically and horizontally, and 'dock' with another jumper in free fall. As an advanced jumper he could then accumulate free fall time at approximately one hour per hundred jumps, with his skill increasing with application.

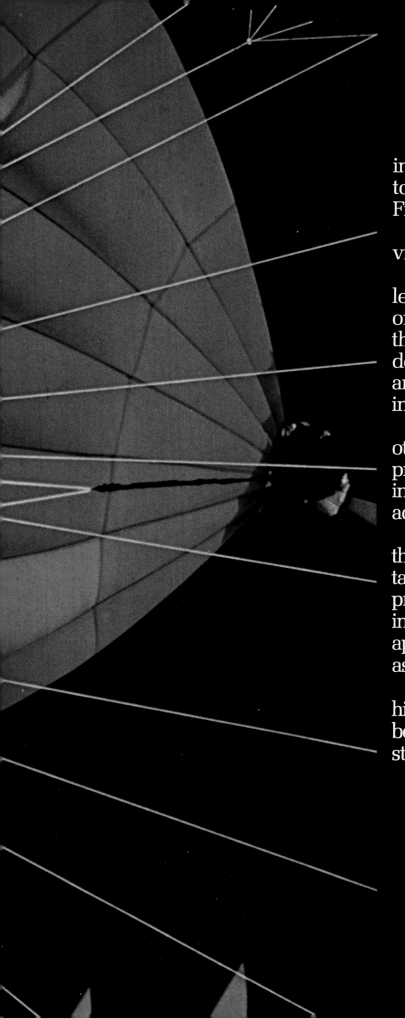

Few sports demand physical involvement for their appreciation to the degree that Free Fall parachuting does.

A dismal spectator activity, viewed at its closest–half a mile.

But every jumper, even the least imaginative, has a collection of visual images burnt into his mind that could never be adequately described in words and, therefore, are lost to all but himself, in an ever fading memory.

Some images are 'stills'; others, in motion; and all are probably technically incorrect, in that the jumper is invariably in an adrenalin-charged state.

A measurable example is that free fall movie film is often taken at a faster speed than it is projected on the screen, in order that the filmed actions appear as graceful and smooth as remembered by the jumper.

In short, a jumper often sees his jump in slow motion because his mind is highly stimulated during the jump.

Still images are infinitely varied
and may include such examples as
the floating sister ship on jump-run,
nose high, in formation
20 yards across the void;
or perhaps, the pained expression
of a 'star' member on realisation
he is about to be rammed;
or a biplane on the top of a loop
with jumper departing,
trailing a long arc of red smoke;
or the confused fluttering of
the jumper's own pilot chute against
his helmet in lazy opening.
     The unique capabilities of
the camera and the written word,
are inseparable from the purpose
of this book–
to express the spirit of the jumper
and preserve the fleeting beautiful
moments and the natural majesty
of the jumpers' playground.

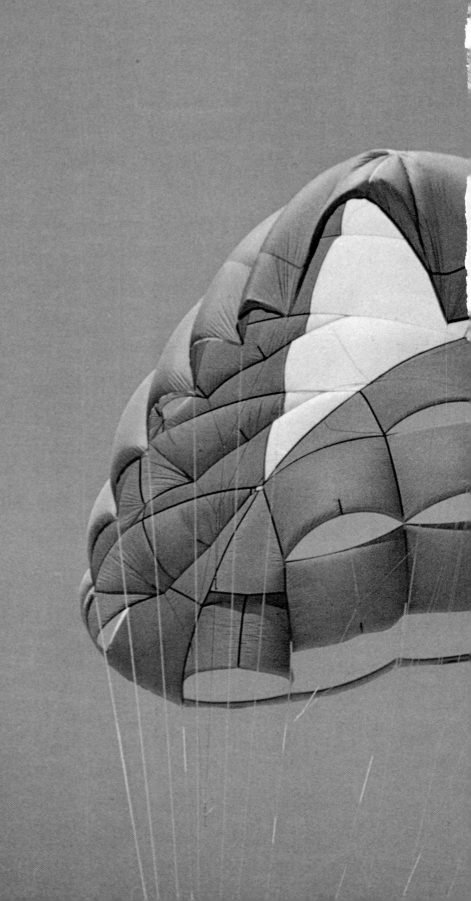

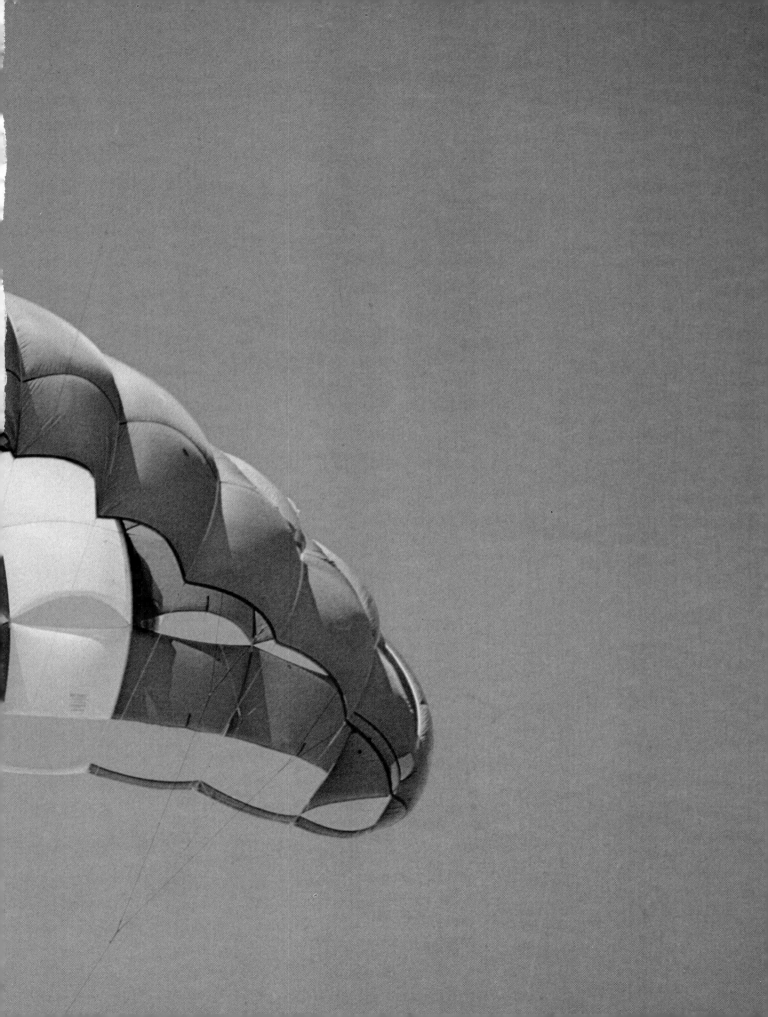

No enduring poetry or writing has yet surfaced from our sport. It would seem surprising to most jumpers that anyone should think it should, or even, think it at all. Yet, aviation nurtures the myth of "dancing the skies on laughter silvered wings" and "touching the face of God," while arm-chair pilots identify with the heroes of Ernest Gann's adventures.

If the world's obsession with "freedom" is more obvious to those without it, perhaps aviators within the confines of their cabins are more inclined to lucid prose. There is little similarity in freedoms of any kind, except that all have limits; the purer the freedom, seemingly, the more limiting parameters. In jumping, these limits are time and distance, as inflexible as extinction. We must enjoy our freedom quickly, but not savour it, except in retrospect.

Perhaps our sport does not lend itself to words as well as it does to visual images. Jumpers seem more inclined to short range instant gratification pursuits than the norm, and less inclined to prolonged introspection.

The work of Capa and Burrows will be long lost in time, while Byron and Shakespeare will be fresh as they are today. So, for all that a picture is worth a thousand words, it depends on the pictures, and the words. While pictures have two dimensions, words have depth, and so does Man.

Either publicly or privately, jumpers are elitist, and beneath the surface of most of these people is a dormant or active competitive spirit. It would follow therefore, that the selection of champions is fiercely contested.

The criteria for selection has been unchanged in over a decade, and involves only two parachuting skills–Style, in a series of simple aerobatic maneouvres in free fall, and Accuracy, to a target under canopy. While this may soon seem tedious to an outsider, its simplicity is in contrast with the dedication required to achieve perfection. An increasing proportion of the leading jumpers are further directing their energies along narrower channels and specialising on one skill or the other.

With competitors from thirty nations now attending World Competition, parachuting is probably the most international single sport, in nations represented. Competition is not a western phenomena. Wherever there are jumpers, there is competition. Whenever there is world competition, the actual attendance of some of the contestants is itself a triumph of dedication to purpose over common sense. While some fully sponsored competitors complain about inadequacies of per diem pocket money, others are peeling potatoes in steerage in an all-out effort to reach the coast line of the host nation.

If winning is only in coming first, competitors have a lot of experience in losing. A man draws his own judgement in what he considers success or failure. For one, second may be a disaster, for another, tenth may be undreamed of success. They have a realistic understanding of their worth and it is in comparison with this estimate that they judge their own performance. The wish to make the comparison is the competitive spirit; to make it is to compete.

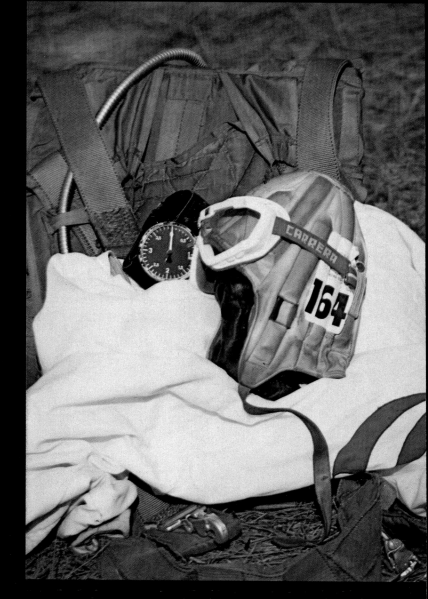

Welcome JUMPERS

164

WORLD CHAMPIONSHIPS
TAHLEQUAH U·S·A 1972
BRITISH PARACHUTE TEAM

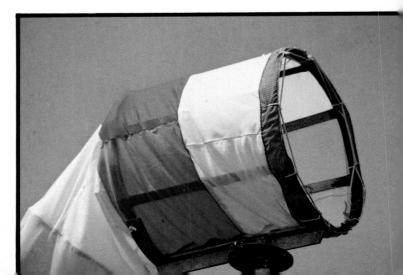

To leave your bed at midnight in search of cooler air
     While your roommate slumbers on, without an obvious care
Your mind's a mile a minute, adrenalin seems to run
     To have his peace of mind and sleep, six hours till next sun.

He hasn't slacked his full pursuit of sports elusive fame
     Or starved imagination to feed his muscled frame
He is tomorrow's favourite, no fate or luck will choose
     Consistent perseverance, and so disinclined to lose

He seems to smell the wind change that won't show on the ground
     And rides the changing windline that others never found
So steady in the saddle, he's listened to his coach
     All runs seem duplicated from the copy-book approach.

But every day is different, no success is guaranteed
     Each point so fiercely fought for with ability and need
So if your inclination is to lead and not be led
     Conserve this tension for tomorrow, retire yourself to bed.

How can I rationalise this fire, that's in my chest now burning?
  The need to win at any cost, and then my private yearning
For world acclaim, to know my name brings instant recognition
  To go afield, to hang one's shield, the Call of competition.

Why must it cost my sleep at night, and cheerful peace of mind?
  Why am I desperately concerned to find myself behind?
Where is the noble selflessness the Greeks were famous for?
  I'd sell my soul, disown a friend, if it would help my score.

What of the opposition, does he know more than I?
  Has he any limitations on just how hard he'll try?
Does he worry that his bones may break and muscles surely bruise?
  Or does he fear far more than that, that he may even lose?

What motivates the other man, is it the same as I?
  The wish to join a culled elite, valhalla of the sky
Perhaps he is just what he seems, behind his easy grin
  An exercise in dedication, with unswerving will to win.

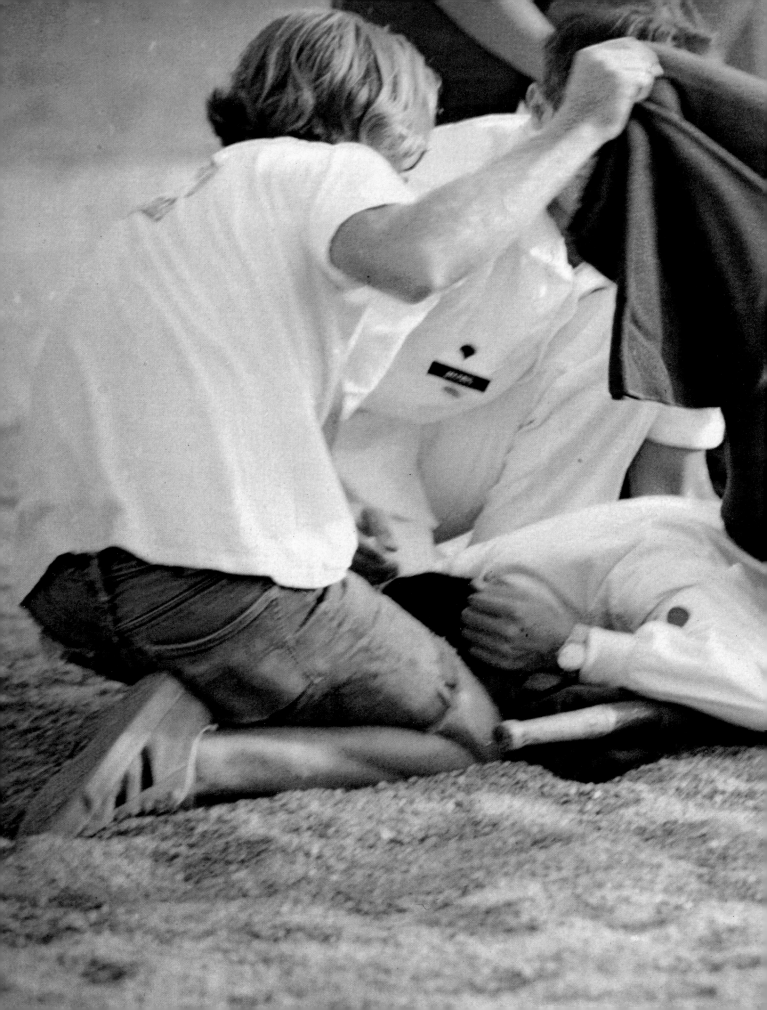

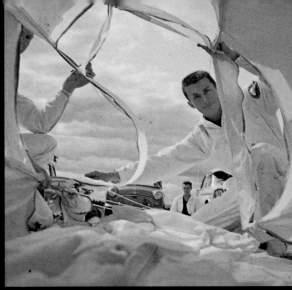

The space that nature offers
    Movement changing to spee
Speed blending with colour
    Colour combined with motio

Parachutists are too varied, flexible and imaginative to find solo competition the only outlet for the pursuit of excellence. It has long been the impression of solo competitors that relative workers were just jumpers without the high motivation to compete. Yet, a year before relative work even reached the status of international competition, the largest parachute competition in registered contestants ever held in the world, was a regional 10 man relative work meet. A lot of competitively-inclined parachutists don't wish to be the world champion in a branch of parachuting they find unexciting and lacking in originality.

The world of the relative worker is a group involvement. He feels the comradeship of team effort, the loyalty to a charismatic leader, the desperation to avoid letting the team down. We have seen the team, drunk with success, walking in with arms full of parachutes, voices raised over each other in instant replay of the event they shared a few minutes before. We have never seen a stylist in a similar euphoria over turning 6.7 seconds. It is all so serious, as if we would spoil the purity of competition if it was enjoyed.

While a solo competitor can enter competition as a beginner with a few jumps, the relative worker is only accepted after demonstration of a fast, safe, and reliable performance in the air, and dependability and compatibility with the group on the ground.

Although solo competition will remain the method to choose the individual world champion, an increasing proportion of the jumping population is moving to the excitement of group formation free fall. In spite of the inconveniences of this activity– the requirement for more altitude, bigger or more aircraft, and the obvious disadvantage of not being able to participate alone, this branch of the sport is mushrooming.

It will be interesting to see the relative importance placed on the two main branches of our sport by 1980.

They proved our hearts beat faster,
    as exit time draws near
Do they feel the graph is showing
    man's self-inflicted fear
Do they smugly say 'he's human' as
    they plot the upward surge
Do they know they're really reading
    a jumper's primal urge?

Have they heard staccato windblast,
    as each man goes through the door
Have they felt his wild excitement
    as his body starts to soar
Can they read exhileration as
    he rolls in slipstream's blast
Or know his pride in star work
    when he makes it tenth
            and last?

Have they burst into the sunlight,
    seen the colours that we know
As we search for clustered bodies,
    of our team mates far below
Then pitching down in clean pursuit
    propelled by urgent need
And feel the air grow stiffer
    in our ever mounting speed.

Have they lived the satisfaction of riding someone's wake
The faster speed, his dumb surprise, then pass to overtake
The giant's hand against the chest, the cushioned flair for air
To hover with the star and know,
at last, you're there.

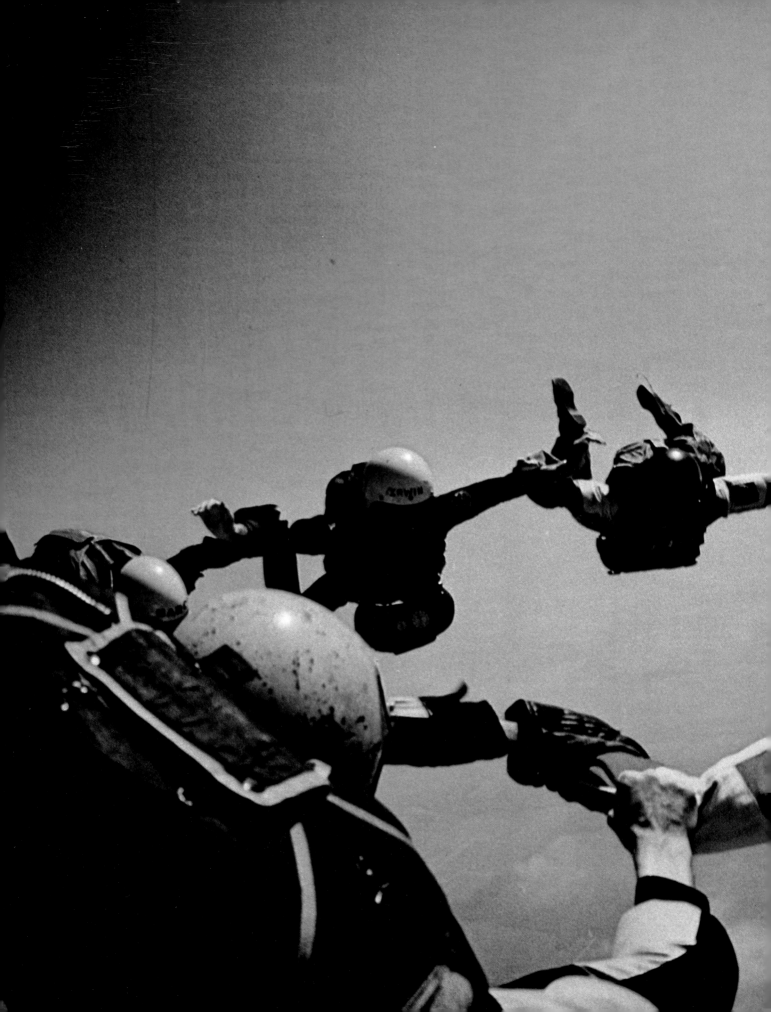

Call "Cut" above the engines drone
a step to windy quiet
Alone

Then sink with elevated feeling
Eternal space, no walls,
No ceiling

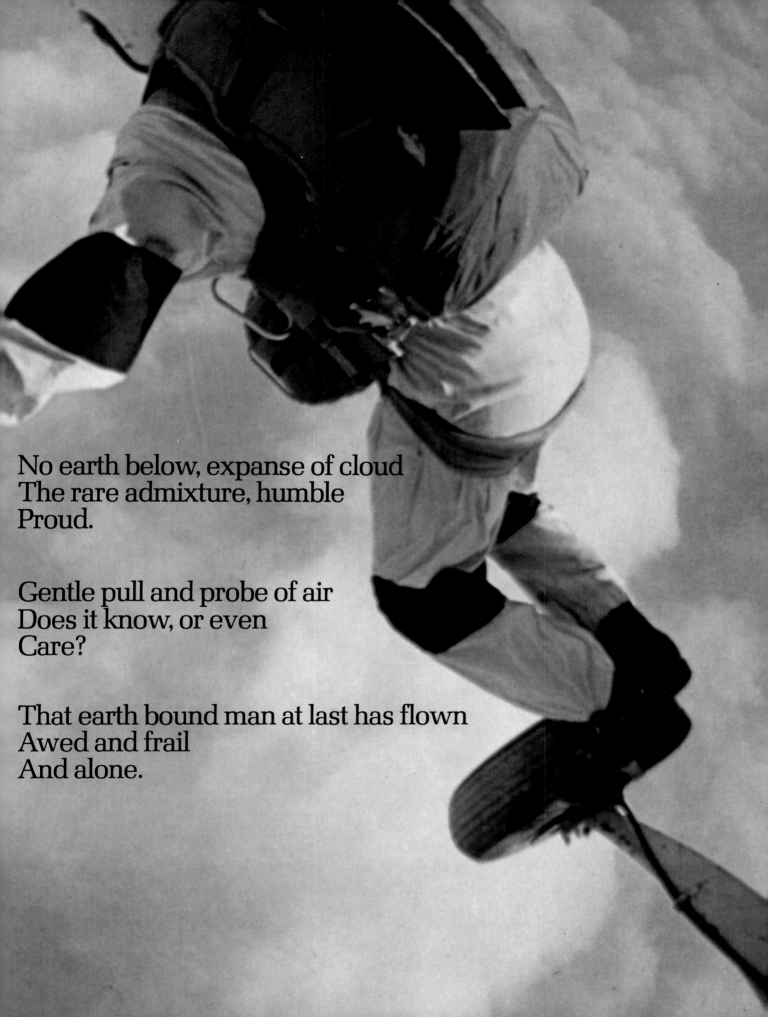

No earth below, expanse of cloud
The rare admixture, humble
Proud.

Gentle pull and probe of air
Does it know, or even
Care?

That earth bound man at last has flown
Awed and frail
And alone.

Jumpers are ordinary and extraordinary in much the way all people are different. We are similar in a low tolerance of neurotic or unrealistic fear in ourselves and others, but we are not without concerns. We worry more about the malfunction of a student than malfunction of his equipment. Human failure, our own and others, is more often responsible for our occasional "close" or disastrous experiences.

We worry little about our equipment; it is honest, mechanically simple and dependable. We are concerned about the real dangers a non-jumper never imagines. Open water below a jumper is probably the most potentially fatal situation, even though there is generally time to respond and survive. Collisions. the simultaneous crossing of flight paths, are different: they happen without warning and sometimes without cure. We are frightened of collisions and the possibility has our full attention.

Collisions may occur between parachutists under canopy; relative speeds are low, with little damage from contact, but there is a high chance of entanglement and collapse of all support required for safe descent to the ground. These collisions generally occur during opening surge or shortly after opening, which allows the maximum amount of time for corrective action.

In free fall, vertical and horizontal differences can produce closing rates of up to 60 m.p.h. We have seen others closing like aerial sharks at full speed, as if homing on some invisible victim.

At low speed the bodies mold together briefly, separating, to quickly regain control. At higher speeds our bodies act less like liquids and more as solids. We tend to ricochet; at the point of impact where inertia and momentum apply their give and take, the shock absorbancy of the body is quickly saturated and exceeded. Air is knocked from the lungs as with some violent body blow, bones break depending on points and direction of contact. A nose is flattened, its cartilage splinters, teeth are pushed through the lower lip and the neck may break as the head rolls to accommodate the momentum of the body following. In free fall, unconsciousness is synonymous with death. We meet, from time to time, some individual who can vaguely remember dribbling out a ripcord handle in a grey descending stupor as his body cartwheeled like some rag doll through the air.

A collision between a man in free fall and an open canopy is the most awesome experience probable to a jumper. An inflated canopy descends at 10 m.p.h.; a man in free fall is a 220lb cannon ball closing at 110 m.p.h.

If he grazes the edge of the canopy, he is fortunate and merely tears a piece from the edge. If he falls within the circumference, the probability of injury approaches certainty. The canopy inverts to accommodate the intrusion, even to the point it is below the jumper it was supporting. The body will blow out of the canopy, severing each quarter ton rigging line it finds in its way, hopefully conscious and functioning. The jumper above has a high probability of falling into his own canopy.

This particular collision becomes more serious as the point of penetration approaches the centre of the canopy. More lines must be broken, as they radiate from the centre. However, the most damage occurs when the jumpers make physical contact. To touch a man's hand at these speeds is to pulverise the bones in that hand. To make body contact with his shoulder will demolish his arm, shoulder and rib cage; there will be pelvic and internal injuries of catastrophic degree.

While these injuries sound similar to those of an automobile accident, they are also similar in their result and seriousness. Our generation has adjusted to accepting the hazard of the highway, in sharing the risk of physical injury with a complete stranger. Yet, jumpers of any calibre will refuse to jump with an unknown. Our attitude is indeed far more conservative towards safety than the initial image of our sport. Consequently, collisions are generally avoidable and fortunately, extremely rare occurrences.

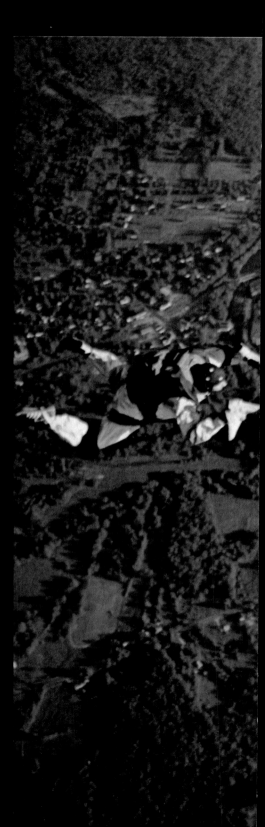

...concern for low fuel level on a busy day... wondering why black liquid is splattering over the windshield...flying all day, knowing no one will think to get you a coke or sandwich... suffering the impatience of overdressed jumpers while insisting fuel <u>is</u> necessary...a sore back... being in ground effect with full load and a disintegrating piston, wondering where it all must go in the very near future...being accepted as a 'cool tool' by the local super jocks...eternal fear of a mid-air...knowing the jump run better than the jumper...hiding behind the control wheel, with a runaway jump door shredding the upholstery... wondering if there'll be a pilot chute over the tail...or through the window...having controls lock in flight...being the only jumper who isn't jumping ...knowing this machine is fatiguing at 4 times the rate of normal aircraft...freezing in the winter... wondering where the comforting noises went to...if there will be be loud and expensive noises later...

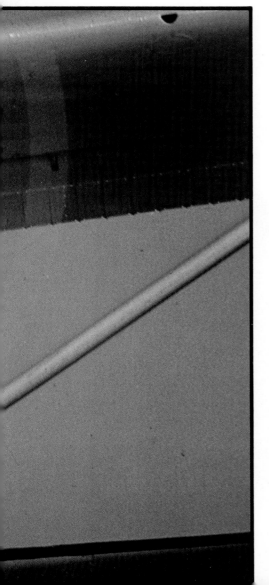

Have you noticed that the camera man is always on the list?
     While others are omitted
     for the last star that they missed
Does he feel a sense of privilege to never miss the ride
     On board he's always welcome,
     he doesn't have to hide.

Have you seen the way he fiddles, with each change in overcast?
     Checking settings and connections,
     that plugs are firm and fast
All this, to freeze the action of our efforts in the sky
     With motor-driven body
     and great glass Cyclope's eye.

He invested family's fortune to own this tiny jewel
     And stressed domestic harmony,
     a wise man or a fool
More weight on mind and shoulders than helmet and his gear
     And gone are all the savings
     for somewhere near a year.

He worries where the light will be, position of the sun
     May even ask to force the spot,
     and make a crosswind run
His openings more violent, his neck will feel the strain
     The week may well be over
     before he's free of pain.

The plane's a mess, U/S
We cannot go without it
A jump today? you guess
I doubt it.

"What do we have?"
"Twelve five, but twelve grand is haze, can't see anything through it."

"We'd best get it down a bit."
"O.K.–take her down."
"Hold it, I have a fix. Twenty left, the field's six miles down range."
"Twenty left, six miles to go!"

"Say gang, I'm showing empty on both."
"There appears to be a gas situation up front. Hell! there goes the port engine. Come on, Bill! Get off your tail. This thing has a ton of jumpers and glides like a brick outhouse!"
"We've lost them both! Get 'em out!

Out! Out! Dammit!"
"Chute, it's a long way home, hope the pilot doesn't have to walk."

Does your woman
sleep in peace
at night
and never stir
in startled fright
from nightmare dreams
of your demise
the pain of terror
in her eyes.

The only pure love is the love one man feels for another

You were more than friends, like brothers,
    than other men I've known
You shared the sky with jumping,
    and the giant planes you've flown
You seemed to share a private joy,
    when the other was around
Both strong and quiet and Texan,
    much in common you'd found.

No love is ever stronger,
    than man holds for the air
What good and noble loyalties
    you two had come to share
I felt admiring envy
    for what you both had done
You accepted me among you,
    in my mind still two and one.

It asks no reward.

The sense of cold foreboding
    we all felt, but brushed aside
No time for superstition as
    we harnessed for the ride
A touchy crosswind takeoff,
    and the jump run made by Dave
No joking in the cabin,
    all quiet and glum and grave.

We cannot court disaster,
    and always stay unscathed
His path to freezing water
    had been steepened and was paved
By canopy collision
    and a cutaway below
No height for safe manoeuvering
    and nowhere else to go.

In the quiet of the evening,
    you know his family's grief
The will to not accept his loss,
    a rage without relief
He was worth too much to lose this way,
    a jump that came to nought
The mistress you must love and hate,
    the mistress called … our sport.

If I could retrieve
    the fortune I have spent
Worrying where it came from,
    not caring where it went
I could live the heady lifestyle
    of Playboy magazine
I would see the worldly sights,
    that still remain unseen.

It must amount to thousands
    I've squandered on the sport
The mark of any jumper,
    a balance close to nought
But if I had it back
    in one financial lump
I'd go south in the winter
    and jump and jump and jump.

Man small.
Why fall?
Skies call.
That's all.

This is his last good season,
I wonder what we'd find
        If we could see the reason,
        and what is on his mind
He started in the Fifties,
        what memories of those years
Of youth and high adventure and experimental fears.

He jumped at small town fairs
after long nights in a train
        Slept with lonely aircraft
        in hangars when it rained
Countless half forgotten faces
        of strangers on the way
A sinking sense of loss when cloud blew low all day

The friendships formed a decade back,
most precious in his mind
        A special type, the selfless few,
        his pioneering kind
He gladly helped his sport mature,
        while every year it's grown
His ranks are sadly thinning, he's practically alone.

What weight is on his shoulders now,
a business, wife or son?
        He'd felt youth was eternal,
        life, everlasting fun
He lived the highest aspirations
        that ever crossed your mind
The meets you hope to jump in, he's already left behind.

His gear still carries dust
from drop zones round the world
        He stood with national team
        and saw his flag unfurled
So if our ranks he now must leave,
        no reason should be sought
Respect his silent privacy, the turmoil of his thought.